TEXAS A&M
AGGIES

BY KEN RAPPOPORT

Published by ABDO Publishing Company, PO Box 398166, Minneapolis, MN 55439. Copyright © 2013 by Abdo Consulting Group, Inc. International copyrights reserved in all countries. No part of this book may be reproduced in any form without written permission from the publisher. SportsZone™ is a trademark and logo of ABDO Publishing Company.

Printed in the United States of America,
North Mankato, Minnesota
102012
012013

Editor: Chrös McDougall
Series Designer: Craig Hinton

Photo Credits: Aaron M. Sprecher/AP Images, cover, 26, 39, 41; David J. Phillip/AP Images, 1; James A. Finley/AP Images, 4; Eric Gay/AP Images, 6, 31, 33, 42 (bottom right); Tom Gannam/AP Images, 9; Mary Butkus/AP Images, 11; Cal Sport Media/AP Images, 12, 42 (top); David J. Phillip/AP Images, 17, 43 (top left), 44; AP Images, 18, 21, 22, 25, 43 (top right); Bettmann/Corbis/AP Images, 29, 42 (bottom left); Stephen Dunn/Getty Images, 34; Brett Coomer/AP Images, 37, 43 (bottom)

Library of Congress Cataloging-in-Publication Data
Rappoport, Ken.
 Texas A&M Aggies / Ken Rappoport.
   p. cm. -- (Inside college football)
Includes bibliographical references and index.
ISBN 978-1-61783-657-2
1. Texas A & M Aggies (Football team)--History--Juvenile literature. 2. Texas A & M University--Football--History--Juvenile literature. I. Title.
796.332--dc15

2012945817

TABLE OF CONTENTS

Texas A&M quarterback Branndon Stewart looks to pass during the 1998 Big 12 Championship Game against Kansas State.

BIG 12 SHOOTOUT

THE TEXAS A&M AGGIES NEEDED A HERO. THE 1998 BIG 12 CONFERENCE FOOTBALL CHAMPIONSHIP WAS AT STAKE. AND IN THE THIRD QUARTER, THE AGGIES TRAILED THE SECOND-RANKED KANSAS STATE WILDCATS BY 15 POINTS. THE 27–12 DEFICIT SEEMED IMPOSSIBLE FOR THE AGGIES TO OVERCOME. TO MAKE MATTERS WORSE, THEIR STARTING QUARTERBACK WAS SIDELINED BY INJURY.

The stakes were huge. In the second quarter, an announcement had come over the loudspeaker. The third-ranked University of California, Los Angeles had just lost. That cleared the way for a spot in the national championship game for the Wildcats. They just had to beat the Aggies.

The Kansas State players slapped high-fives on the sidelines. "It gave us a lift," confessed Wildcats lineman Jeremy Martin.

It also gave a lift to the purple-clad Kansas State fans among the 60,000 in attendance at the Trans World Dome in

St. Louis. They cheered. The Aggies, meanwhile, were not playing for the national championship. But a Big 12 title would propel them into a major bowl game.

Playing in bowl games was nothing new for the Aggies. They had a rich tradition in that regard. The Aggies had played in 33 bowl games through 2011. That included eight since 2000.

The 1939 Aggie team won the national championship with a victory over Tulane in the Sugar Bowl. In addition, the Aggies had won 17 titles in the Southwest Conference before joining the Big 12 in 1996.

The Aggies had produced some of college football's greatest players, including Heisman Trophy winner John David Crow in 1957. And now the team was looking to add to its legacy in 1998 against a tough Kansas State team in the Big 12 Championship Game. The Wildcats had won the North Division with an undefeated record. They were heavily favored to beat the Aggies—the South champions.

The game followed expectations early on. Time was running out on the underdog Aggies. Then they found their hero.

The Aggies placed their hopes in the hands of senior Branndon Stewart—a quarterback with an up-and-down career. Stewart had once played for the Tennessee Volunteers. He served as a backup to future National Football League star Peyton Manning before transferring to Texas A&M. Stewart was required to sit out a year after switching schools. Then he had trouble keeping the starting quarterback position through 1997 and 1998.

MILITARY TRADITIONS

For much of its history, Texas A&M was a military school. Originally named Agricultural College of Texas at its founding in 1876, the school became Texas Agricultural & Mechanical (A&M) University in 1963. Also during the 1960s, the school began admitting women and minorities. And it no longer required students to participate in the Corps of Cadets. However, the Corps remains the largest uniformed body of students outside the service academies. Texas A&M continues to turn out commissioned officers for all of the military services.

DAT NGUYEN

It was a dangerous journey. Dat Nguyen (pronounced "win"), the great Aggies linebacker of the 1990s, was not yet born. His family was fleeing Saigon in the midst of the Vietnam War. In the middle of the night, Nguyen's family boarded a fishing boat. Three months later, they found themselves in the United States, where Nguyen was born.

The family settled in Rockport, Texas. Nguyen played football at Rockport-Fulton High School. He was highly recruited but decided to stay close to home. "I just woke up one day and said, 'I'm an Aggie,'" Nguyen said.

Nguyen played big despite a relatively small size for a linebacker. He was just 5-foot-11 and 231 pounds. He played so big, in fact, that he had a team record 517 career tackles. That included 17 in the Aggies' upset of Kansas State in the 1998 Big 12 Championship Game. As a senior in 1998, he won the Lombardi Award as the nation's top collegiate lineman.

But starting quarterback Randy McCown was injured in a loss to Texas in the final game of the 1998 season. So Stewart was forced to take over.

Stewart went to work in the fourth quarter. He drove Texas A&M 78 yards down the field. He then found junior wide receiver Leroy Hodge on a 13-yard touchdown pass with 9:20 left. That brought the Aggies within eight points, by a score of 27–19. The game was within reach.

But now Kansas State had possession of the ball. It had a chance to close out the game with less than three minutes remaining. Wildcats quarterback Michael Bishop appeared to pick up the first down that would have run out the clock.

Aggies senior linebacker Warrick Holdman had a different idea. He knocked the ball loose. And his teammate—sophomore linebacker Cornelius Anthony—recovered it on the 35-yard line for Texas A&M.

The Texas A&M Aggies go after the Kansas State offense during the 1998 Big 12 Championship Game.

"It was just a sick feeling," said Bishop, who had otherwise had a brilliant game.

Bishop had thrown for 341 yards and two touchdowns and run for another. Stewart had to work fast. The Aggies started on the 50-yard line. Stewart completed a 36-yard pass to junior receiver Matt Bumgardner on first down. It was Bumgardner's only catch of the day.

On third and nine from the 9-yard line, Stewart connected with senior Sirr Parker. The Aggies' second-team running back caught the pass for a touchdown to cut the Kansas State lead to 27–25.

[9]

Stewart again went to Parker on a two-point conversion to tie the score at 27 each with 1:05 left in regulation.

"I'm only 5-11, but I was 6 feet on that one," said Parker as the game went into overtime.

In overtime, each team starts at the 25-yard line with a first down. Teams can score either by a touchdown or a field goal. Or they can give up the ball on downs.

In the first overtime, the Aggies went ahead 30–27 on a field goal by Russell Bynum. But the Wildcats' kicker followed by booting a 22-yard field goal. The game was tied at 30.

So it went into a second overtime. Kansas State kicked another field goal—this one from 25 yards. The Wildcats moved in front 33–30. Texas A&M had the chance to match with another field goal or win with a touchdown. It was an opportunity for Stewart to be the hero.

The Aggies lost two yards on the first play of their possession. A penalty moved them back even farther. They faced a third-and-17 play. It was going to be all or nothing for Stewart.

"WRECKING CREW"

Former Aggies safety Chet Brooks was watching a game tape during the 1980s. When he saw Texas A&M's high-powered defense, the nickname was obvious. He coined the term the "Wrecking Crew." "That was just the way we played then," Brooks said. "We said we were wrecking them." The nickname—one of the most famous in college football—is still in effect today.

The Aggies decided not to go for the tie this time. They went for the touchdown. Stewart fired another pass to Parker, who gathered it in and sidestepped a Wildcats defender. With one final push Stewart made it into the end zone.

The final score was Texas A&M 36, Kansas State 33. The Wildcats' loss knocked them out of the national championship game. It dropped them to a lower-level bowl. The final play of the game meanwhile propelled Texas A&M into the prestigious Sugar Bowl. The play is regarded as one of the greatest in A&M football history—just another highlight in a glorious football story.

[11]

Kyle Field at Texas A&M will always be known as the home of the "12th Man."

2

THE "12TH MAN"

 A STUDENT WAS ABOUT TO BECOME A LEGEND AT TEXAS A&M. E. K. GILL WAS TO BECOME THE "12TH MAN."

It was January 2, 1922—46 years after Texas A&M opened and 28 years after the school fielded its first football team. Gill's day had started with a climb up to the press box high in the grandstand to witness the Dixie Classic. The Classic, a bowl game played in Dallas, featured a battle between the Aggies and powerful Centre College. The Classic later became known as the Cotton Bowl.

Gill was a former Aggies football player. He had quit the sport to play basketball. But now he was back to assist the football team. Players at that time did not wear numbers or names on their uniforms. So Gill had been asked to go to the press box to help sportswriters identify the players.

The Aggies were not given much of a chance against the powerhouse team from Kentucky. The undefeated Praying

Colonels were 20-point favorites. According to the *New York Times*, "The Aggies will take the field outweighed 13 pounds to the man."

It did not seem to bother the Aggies, though. They took a 2–0 lead in the first three minutes of play. The Aggies' defense was at its best. In the second quarter, Centre needed only a foot to make a first down. But the Colonels failed on two chances.

The teams went into the third quarter with Texas A&M still clinging to a 2–0 lead. But the great defensive battle began to take its toll on the Aggies. They suffered a number of injuries, which included a broken leg for captain Heinie Weir.

The Aggies' squad was down to a precious few. Coach Dana X. Bible was desperate. Gill, still in the press box, was called to come down to the field.

"Boy, it looks like we may not have enough players to finish the game," Bible told Gill. "You may have to go in and stand around for a while."

"Yes, sir," Gill responded eagerly.

The rules were different then. To be eligible to play, a player only had to attend class for one day before a game.

Gill did not realize at this point that he would be starting a tradition that is still going today. He was the "12th Man," always ready to help the team.

There were no locker rooms in stadiums at that time. The team had dressed downtown at the hotel and traveled to the stadium in taxicabs. Gill had to change clothes. So he and Weir ducked underneath the stands. Aggies tackle Tiny Keen remembered how players held up a blanket so that Gill could change clothes with Weir. Gill was now wearing Weir's uniform, and Weir was wearing Gill's street clothes.

Gill waited on the sidelines to be called into the game. In the second half, the Praying Colonels took a 7–2 lead on a three-yard touchdown run by Jack Snoddy and the extra-point kick. But the Aggies came back. Running back Puny Wilson tossed a touchdown pass to Jack Evans. An extra point made it 9–7 in favor of Texas A&M.

A crowd of 20,000 at Fair Park Stadium cheered when Wilson later scored on a five-yard run for Texas A&M. The Aggies built their lead to 16–7. Gill, the only substitute available for the Aggies, was still waiting to be called.

The Aggies made it 22–7 when Aggies tackle Ted Winn intercepted a pass and returned it 45 yards for a touchdown. Centre was stunned. The team had given up only six points to its opponents for an entire season. Now it had allowed 22 points in a single game.

The Colonels mounted one last drive, scoring a touchdown late in the game. But it was too little, too late. Texas A&M went on to a shocking 22–14 victory over Centre.

Gill ended up not having to play. But it was regarded as one of the greatest upsets in college football history. By then, the Aggies already had a rich history that featured the coaching of Charley Moran and Bible. Since the beginning of football at Texas A&M in 1894, the Aggies had won three conference championships.

Moran coached the Aggies from 1909 to 1914. He recorded one of the best records in school history until that time at 38–8–4.

Bible produced powerhouses in 1917 and 1919 that were not only unbeaten, but unscored upon. The 1917 team went 8–0 and outscored opponents 270–0. The 1919 team won each of its 10 games, outscoring opponents 275–0.

In 1922, the "12th Man" expression became a part of Aggies tradition. Harry "Red" Thompson, part of the strong student support system, used the phrase for the first time in describing Gill.

CROSS THE LINE

Coach Dana X. Bible had to do something. It was halftime of the 1922 battle with archrival Texas. The Aggies were tied 7–7 with the Longhorns. So Bible dragged his foot across the floor of the Texas A&M locker room. "Those who want to go out and be known as members of an A&M team that defeated Texas in Austin, step over the line." The entire team rushed across the line and then went out and beat Texas 14–7.

Gill's role was vital. His readiness to play or help in any other way seemed to inspire his teammates. "He was ready," noted Keen. "That's the point."

Today, visiting teams at Kyle Field in College Station, Texas, cannot help but notice the massive sign, "Home of the 12th Man." Nor can they help but notice that A&M students stand for the entire game. It is another traditional practice that symbolized their willingness to help.

"I wish I could say that I went in and ran for the winning touchdown, but I did not," Gill recalled in later years. "I simply stood by in case my team needed me."

That was enough.

Coach Homer Norton had an 82–53–9 record for Texas A&M from 1934 to 1947, including a 2–2 record in bowl games.

3

NATIONAL CHAMPIONS

AGGIES COACH HOMER NORTON SURVEYED HIS PLAYERS AS THE 1939 FOOTBALL SEASON APPROACHED. COULD THIS BE THE TEAM HE WAS LOOKING FOR—THE BEST HE HAD COACHED IN SIX YEARS?

Norton was a coach known for his powerful offense and superb defense. From 1926 to 1933, while coaching at Centenary College, he never had a losing season. Since taking over as the Aggies' football coach in 1934, however, his teams had struggled.

But now the present looked brighter. The Aggies featured fullback "Jarrin" John Kimbrough. The *New York Times* called him one of the most destructive fullbacks the game has known.

Kimbrough, a native of Haskell, Texas, was known locally as the "Haskell Hurricane." He accepted a football scholarship to Tulane, but he was unhappy at the New Orleans school. Coaches there wanted him to play tackle. But Kimbrough liked to carry the ball. So he transferred to Texas A&M to play for the Aggies.

It was 1938 and the fourth game of the season. Texas A&M was playing the powerful Texas Christian University (TCU) Horned Frogs. TCU was on its way to the national championship. The Aggies were taking a beating and no one wanted to carry the ball. That is, no one except Kimbrough. By this time, the sophomore had developed his powerful 6-foot-2, 210-pound frame into an unstoppable force.

Time and again, Kimbrough smashed into the TCU line without fear. On one play, a TCU player was carried off the field after getting hit by Kimbrough. Although the Aggies lost the game, Kimbrough received praise from his teammates for his efforts.

Kimbrough was back in 1939. The Aggies opened that season by beating Oklahoma A&M—now Oklahoma State—by a score of 32–0. Then the Aggies shut out Centenary College 14–0. And a 7–3 victory over a powerful Santa Clara team brought national attention to the Aggies.

HOMER NORTON

Aggies coach Homer Norton preferred to sit in the press box rather than stand on the sidelines for games. He would scream and yell as he watched the game. There was little to cheer for in 1938 when Norton's Aggies were struggling. His job was on the line in the midst of a 4–4–1 season, and he was highly criticized. Norton felt better in 1939 when his team won the national championship. Then he received praise and a raise.

Texas A&M's star fullback John Kimbrough (39), shown in 1940, also played defense for the Aggies.

In a mid-October game, the Aggies crushed undefeated Villanova 33–7. Kimbrough scored two touchdowns in the game. First he blasted into the middle of the line from two yards out. That showed his power. Then he showed his speed, racing around the end for another touchdown. Kimbrough even caught a pass for a touchdown in Texas A&M's next game, a 20–6 win over TCU.

The Aggies continued to cut up the opposition. Led by their backfield star, the Aggies beat Baylor 20–0, Arkansas 27–0, Southern Methodist 6–2, Rice 9–0, and Texas 20–0.

NATIONAL CHAMPIONS

The next stop for the Aggies was the Sugar Bowl. The Aggies took their number-one ranking and 10–0 record into New Orleans to face Tulane—the local power.

The Associated Press (AP) took note of the fierce Aggies offense sparked by their top runner: "Kimbrough . . . crashed into the renowned Tulane line with power that had never been seen in these parts."

Kimbrough slashed 11 yards for a touchdown to give the Aggies a 7–0 lead in the first quarter.

"Aggie pass plays clicked and the [Tulane] Green Wave, stopped once on the 6-yard line by a surging line, seemed unable to start its power rolling," reported the AP.

It was not until six minutes had passed in the third quarter that Tulane finally got going. Bob Kellogg fielded a punt for Tulane and took off down the sideline. Aggies guard Marshall Robnett went after him. Robnett got his hands on Kellogg, hung on for five yards, and then slipped off.

Four more Aggies were knocked off their feet as Kellogg raced 75 yards for a touchdown. The score was tied 7–7.

Suddenly, Tulane got another big break. A lateral pass from Texas A&M halfback Derace Moser struck Kimbrough's huge hands and bounced crazily on the sidelines. Players flew from everywhere after the ball. Tulane finally came up with it on the Aggies' 38-yard line. The Green Wave then drove for a touchdown. Tulane led 13–7.

James Thibault lined up to kick the extra point. But Herbie Smith, the Aggies' little 160-pound end, had a different idea. He drove in and blocked the extra-point attempt. The Texas A&M backers in the crowd of 73,000 cheered.

Back came Texas A&M. Little Herbie, who had robbed Tulane of the extra point, then took the kickoff and returned it to the Aggies' 31-yard line. The Aggies steadily drove down the field. Going into the middle of the big Tulane line on one play, Kimbrough drove for 18 yards to the Tulane 26-yard line.

BEVO

One of the most memorable stories in the Texas-Texas A&M rivalry involved the Texas mascot, which is a live longhorn steer. It was 1916. In a sneak attack on the Texas campus, Texas A&M students stole the mascot. Then they carried out their devilish plan. They branded the Texas steer with the score of the Aggies' 13–0 victory over the Longhorns in 1915. That game was the first one in the new Southwest Conference.

The Texas students were outraged. So they came up with a solution. They changed the 13–0 brand to read, "BEVO." This is how the Texas mascot was named.

Texas A&M students again stole Bevo and brought him back to College Station in 1963. Then the Texas Rangers got involved. The Rangers are a law enforcement division that investigates crimes throughout Texas. They found Bevo and returned him to a student group that takes care of him.

On the next play, quarterback Cotton Price drifted back and threw a pass to Smith. The Aggies' end then lateraled to Kimbrough, who started toward the goal line.

"Tulane players fell like ten pins [as at a bowling alley] as Kimbrough lowered his head and waded ten yards for the touchdown," the AP reported. Price kicked the extra point to give the Aggies a 14–13 lead.

The Aggies held on to win. It was their first and—through 2011—only national championship. Kimbrough played a major role in securing the victory. He scored two touchdowns and rushed for 159 yards on 25 carries.

As a senior in 1940, Kimbrough finished second in the Heisman Trophy race as the top college football player in the country. Michigan halfback Tom Harmon won the trophy that year. The Aggies would have to wait until 1957 to produce a Heisman winner when running back John David Crow won.

Texas A&M closed out the 1940 season with a victory over Fordham in the Cotton Bowl.

In 1940, the Aggies had a perfect record until the last game of the regular season. That is when archrival Texas came along to spoil their year. Even though the Aggies won the Cotton Bowl game against Fordham, the stinging defeat by the Longhorns at the end of the season had cost them another national championship. And the rivalry would only continue.

NATIONAL CHAMPIONS

The Texas A&M-Texas game, usually played on Thanksgiving, was often one of the most heated games of the year.

4

RED-HOT RIVALRY

GGIES AND LONGHORNS. LONGHORNS AND AGGIES. THEY LOVE BEATING UP ON EACH OTHER.

It started in 1894, when Texas beat Texas A&M 38–0. For more than 100 years after that, their rivalry was one of the most powerful in college football. It was an annual Thanksgiving tradition for many Texans.

On the field, the rivalry came of age in the 1920 game. Both Texas and Texas A&M were undefeated. The Aggies had outscored opponents 226–0. They had not allowed a single point since the last game of the 1918 season. But Texas changed that. The Aggies allowed the Longhorns to cross their goal line. The final score was 7–0. It was Texas A&M's first loss in 19 games.

In 1940, it happened again. The Aggies were on their way to another undefeated season after their national championship. But Texas again won by a score of 7–0.

JOHN DAVID CROW

Before he was a football star, John David Crow was a fan. "Doak Walker was my idol when I was in junior high," Crow said. Walker played for Southern Methodist and Crow wanted to follow him there. By the time Crow was in his senior year of high school, though, he decided to go to Texas A&M. The reason was that coaching master Bear Bryant was there.

"I knew he'd be building and that I could learn faster under him, because he'd be concentrating on the freshmen," Crow said. "In fact, we had such a good freshman team that we beat the varsity."

By the time Crow was a senior at Texas A&M in 1957, he was the talk of the country. The 6-foot-2, 217-pound running back won the Heisman Trophy. And by then, Bryant was a fan of Crow's. "Crow is the greatest back I ever coached," said Bryant, who later set coaching records in a great career at Alabama.

The Aggies were 8–0 when they met Texas in 1941. But Texas won that game 23–0. It was a frustrating era for Aggies fans. Their biggest rival had just ended their national title dreams two seasons in a row. And more frustration was soon to come.

Under coach Homer Norton, the Aggies had losing seasons in 1942, 1946, and 1947. Then Harry Stiteler took over in 1948 and the Aggies went 0–9–1. Between 1946 and 1973, the Aggies had 22 losing seasons.

The highlight of that era was from 1954 to 1957, when coach Paul "Bear" Bryant was in charge. After starting 1–9–0, he led the Aggies to three winning seasons. In 1956, Texas A&M beat Texas 34–21 at Texas' Memorial Stadium. The Aggies had not won there in 16 previous games. That ended up being the best season under Bryant. The team went 9–0–1.

The Aggies were still good in 1957. Running back John David Crow won the

Heisman Trophy that year. The Aggies went 8–3 and earned an invitation to the Gator Bowl. At one point they were ranked number one in the nation. But Bryant left after that season to coach Alabama, where he became legendary.

The Aggies finally turned things around after Emory Bellard took over as coach in 1972. He led the team to 10–2 records in 1975 and 1976. However, he resigned after starting 4–2 in 1978.

The Lone Star Showdown between Texas and Texas A&M was one of the hottest rivalries in college football. But the competition had largely

RED-HOT RIVALRY

cooled off after Texas A&M's 1939 national title. The Longhorns went 36–7–1 against the Aggies from 1940 to 1983. But under third-year coach Jackie Sherrill, Texas A&M turned it around in 1984.

Texas was ranked thirteenth in the country, while Texas A&M was out of the rankings. But the Aggies were not intimidated. They pulled off a 37–12 upset. It was the first of six consecutive wins against the Longhorns. In fact, the Aggies lost to Texas just once in the next 11 seasons.

New coach R. C. Slocum had taken over in 1989. He started 5–1 against Texas. And it was not just Texas that the Aggies were beating. Under Slocum, the Aggies regained their position as a national power. They won 10 or more games five times during the 1990s under Slocum. The Aggies also went to eight bowl games during the decade and were usually ranked among the nation's top 25 teams. And the Aggies were nearly unbeatable at home. Texas A&M lost just four home games during the 1990s.

However, the century ended on a sad note for Texas A&M and for the Lone Star Showdown. Beginning in 1909, Texas A&M students had held a traditional bonfire and massive rally on campus before the Texas game. Scores of students would climb on top of a tower of logs, where an outhouse was placed. It was painted with the Texas color—a burnt orange.

In 1999, different student groups worked 24 hours a day during "Push Week" to build that year's tower. In the early morning hours

one day, students heard a large crack. The heavy logs and poles then came crashing down on them. It was an unbelievable tragedy. Twelve students died and dozens of others were injured.

For a change, football took a back seat on the Texas A&M campus. Never mind the big rivalry game with Texas.

"A lot of guys felt like they couldn't practice," said Aggies junior linebacker Roylin Bradley. "It was like it was our brothers, because we're a part of the A&M family."

The Texas A&M community was not sure if the team would play the game. The Aggies missed two days of practice. But the officials decided the game would go on.

"It was a weird time, you know?" said Texas A&M freshman wide receiver Greg Porter. "You're getting ready to play a football game, and the team on the other side is actually being nice."

A record crowd of 86,128 filled Kyle Field. It was the largest crowd ever to see a football game in Texas to that point. Thousands of maroon balloons, followed by 12 white doves, filled the air. Four F-16 fighter planes flew overhead. It was game time.

The Aggies took an early lead, but the Longhorns led 16–6 at the half. Defense came to the Aggies' rescue in the second half, however. Under his game jersey, Aggies junior left guard Chris Valletta wore the names of the 12 fallen students on a T-shirt. "We thought of them every play," he said.

Nevertheless, the Aggies still trailed late in the third quarter. Then, with 4:47 left in the quarter, Texas A&M junior tailback Ja'Mar Toombs scored his second touchdown of the game. That cut the Longhorns' lead to 16–13.

YELL LEADERS

At Texas A&M, students are taught to yell, and yell loudly. At midnight before each home game, students take part in Midnight Yell. Yell Leaders lead the Fightin' Texas Aggie Band into the stadium. Then they lead the crowd in old army yells and the school's songs.

The Texas A&M community came together following the 1999 bonfire collapse.

Aggies senior quarterback Randy McCown then fired a touchdown pass for the team's winning points. The final score was Texas A&M 20, Texas 16.

"It was the most emotional game I've ever played in my life," said Texas A&M freshman linebacker Brian Gamble.

Texas A&M linebacker Dat Nguyen tackles Missouri's quarterback during a 1998 game at Kyle Field.

5

BOWL SEASON

ALTHOUGH THE AGGIES WERE STILL TRYING FOR THEIR SECOND NATIONAL CHAMPIONSHIP, THE TEAM AGAIN HAD BECOME A NATIONAL POWER UNDER COACH R. C. SLOCUM.

Slocum's first season in charge was 1989. Through 2000, he never had a losing season. And during that time, the team won three Southwest Conference championships. After joining the new Big 12 Conference in 1996, the Aggies earned another league title in 1998. The Aggies also had gone to 10 bowl games under Slocum.

But suddenly, Slocum's job security came into question. Before Slocum was hired at Texas A&M, a cheating scandal had rocked the school. It involved payoffs to players, which was against the rules. Under Slocum, there was no such thing as win at all costs.

"I wouldn't trade winning another game or two for my reputation as a person," he said.

R. C. SLOCUM

R. C. Slocum was more than just a football coach to his players. He valued education along with sports. He was the first person in his family to graduate from college. As a child, he lived in a section of town known as the projects in Orange, Texas. "We were limited in where we could live because we didn't have any money," Slocum remembered.

His father was a hard worker who did not have an education. "I can identify with the kid who grew up poor," Slocum said. Education allowed Slocum to rise to the top of the football world and befriend a US president. President George H. W. Bush and his wife Barbara watched Aggies games in Slocum's suite at Kyle Field.

Slocum knew the importance of an education for his players. "Football's a fleeting thing. If I let him miss the educational opportunities, I've let him down," Slocum said.

His teams did it the right way, with no cheating. However, something happened in 2000 that had never before happened under Slocum. The Aggies lost three games in a row in a single season. They were leading Oklahoma, and then suddenly the lead was gone. The Aggies' archrival Texas crushed Texas A&M by 26 points. Then in the snowy Independence Bowl, the Aggies went into overtime and lost to Mississippi State.

Slocum was a hot topic on talk radio. Fans were angry. They called for Slocum's job. But the coach was not worried.

"If we do the right things for the right reasons, then we'll win enough games to keep our job," Slocum said.

Texas A&M also lost three in a row in 2001 before finishing 8–4. Then the Aggies started the 2002 season 5–4. They were threatening to match their worst season under Slocum. A big game was coming up against Oklahoma, the

nation's top-ranked team. No one gave Texas A&M a chance to win. And no one expected what happened next.

Slocum benched his starting quarterback late in the first quarter. He put the ball in the hands of a freshman, Reggie McNeal. The young quarterback had a tough job ahead of him. Many of the Aggies' key players were injured.

McNeal fired two touchdown passes in the second quarter as the Aggies rallied from a 10–0 deficit to a 13–13 tie at the half. A mostly maroon-clad crowd of 84,036 at Kyle Field cheered as they watched the exciting, back-and-forth game. McNeal was in a groove.

BOWL SEASON

AGGIES

The Aggies went ahead 20–13 when McNeal tossed a 17-yard touchdown pass. But back came Oklahoma to tie the score at 20. The Sooners then kicked a field goal to take the lead.

McNeal was cool under pressure. He connected with sophomore wide receiver Terrence Murphy on a 40-yard touchdown play. The Aggies took back the lead 27–23.

By the time the game was over, the Aggies were in front 30–26. McNeal finished with four touchdown passes and 191 passing yards. The Aggies had pulled off the biggest upset of the season—perhaps of many seasons. They beat a top-ranked team for the first time in Aggies history.

"It's gratifying to go in and play with the number-one team in a game where virtually no one gave us a chance to win," Slocum said. "This is pretty big."

But it was not big enough to save Slocum's job. A loss to Missouri and a 50–20 beating by archrival Texas sealed Slocum's fate. He was

TRADITIONS

Tradition plays a big role in why so many people love college football. Texas A&M has many famous traditions. One of the most honored traditions is Silver Taps. It is a ceremony held for a student who passes away while enrolled at the school. Another tradition involves Reveille, the school mascot, who is the revered dog on campus. If she is sleeping on a cadet's bed, that cadet must sleep on the floor. Cadets address Reveille as "Miss Rev, ma'am." If she is in class and barks while the professor is teaching, the class is to be immediately dismissed.

fired. The coach with the most victories in Aggies football history had become history.

After Slocum, a number of Aggies football coaches followed. The Aggies experienced some success. Coach Dennis Franchione led the team to three bowl games between 2004 and 2007. Behind star linebacker Von Miller, the Aggies went to back-to-back bowl games in 2009 and 2010. Coach Mike Sherman was then fired during a 6–6 regular season in 2011. Tim DeRuyter took over as interim coach.

It had been a difficult year for the Aggies. Sherman was fired on December 1. Just a few weeks later, Texas A&M senior offensive lineman Joseph Villavisencio was killed in a car accident.

BOWL SEASON

"It's been a long year with a lot of ups and downs," said senior quarterback Ryan Tannehill.

The Aggies came into the season thinking about a conference title and a major bowl game. Instead they headed to the Meineke Car Care Bowl. Facing Northwestern in the bowl game, the Aggies players wore black and white decals honoring their fallen teammate. They also dedicated the game to their fired coach.

Behind Tannehill, the Aggies raced to a 33–22 victory over Northwestern. Tannehill threw for 329 yards and a touchdown. It amounted to a virtual home game for the Aggies at Reliant Stadium in Houston.

It still was not the season Texas A&M players and fans had hoped for. But they looked forward to a new era beginning in 2012. That year, the Aggies and the Missouri Tigers left the Big 12 for the Southeastern Conference (SEC). The new conference meant Texas and Texas A&M would suspend their rivalry. The last year in which they did not play each

SACRED GROUNDS

The grounds at Kyle Field are considered sacred. They are dedicated to 55 Aggies who died in World War II. Fifty-five American flags fly at every home game. In Aggies tradition, only people associated with the football team are allowed on the field. During one game, an opposing cheerleader bounced onto the turf. She was roughly turned away by a saber-wielding corpsman. The cadet was restrained and later apologized.

other was 1914. But the SEC was considered the nation's most powerful conference, so the Aggies could not pass up the opportunity to join.

The Aggies also had a new leader as they began the SEC era. Kevin Sumlin was hired as coach before the 2012 season. The landscape of college football was changing. But one thing would never change as far as the Aggies were concerned. Their "12th Man" would always be ready to play.

TIMELINE

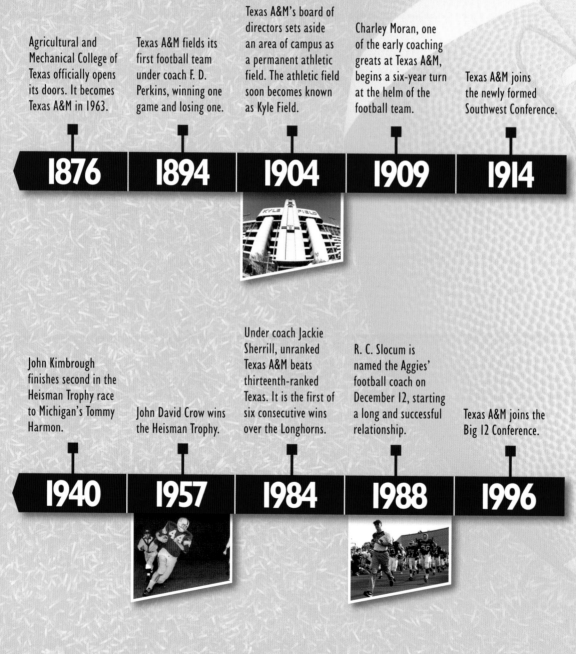

Agricultural and Mechanical College of Texas officially opens its doors. It becomes Texas A&M in 1963.

Texas A&M fields its first football team under coach F. D. Perkins, winning one game and losing one.

Texas A&M's board of directors sets aside an area of campus as a permanent athletic field. The athletic field soon becomes known as Kyle Field.

Charley Moran, one of the early coaching greats at Texas A&M, begins a six-year turn at the helm of the football team.

Texas A&M joins the newly formed Southwest Conference.

1876 **1894** **1904** **1909** **1914**

John Kimbrough finishes second in the Heisman Trophy race to Michigan's Tommy Harmon.

John David Crow wins the Heisman Trophy.

Under coach Jackie Sherrill, unranked Texas A&M beats thirteenth-ranked Texas. It is the first of six consecutive wins over the Longhorns.

R. C. Slocum is named the Aggies' football coach on December 12, starting a long and successful relationship.

Texas A&M joins the Big 12 Conference.

1940 **1957** **1984** **1988** **1996**

The first Southwest Conference game is played at College Station on November 19 as Texas A&M upsets Texas 13–0.

Dana X. Bible joins the Aggies' coaching staff and promptly leads the team to an undefeated season and the Southwest Conference title.

The "12th Man" tradition at Texas A&M begins during a victory in the Dixie Classic in Dallas on January 2.

Homer Norton takes over as the Texas A&M football coach.

The Aggies win the national championship, capping the season with a victory over Tulane in the Sugar Bowl.

1915   **1917**   **1922**   **1934**   **1939**

THE 12TH MAN

Texas A&M wins the Big 12 title with a 36–33 overtime victory over Kansas State on December 5.

Twelve A&M students die in a collapse of the traditional bonfire before the Texas game.

On November 9, the Aggies stun top-ranked Oklahoma in one of the greatest upsets in school history.

In coach Mike Sherman's last season, Texas A&M goes 7–6. Kevin Sumlin is hired as Sherman's replacement.

Texas A&M splits from the Big 12 to join the SEC.

1998   **1999**   **2002**   **2011**   **2012**

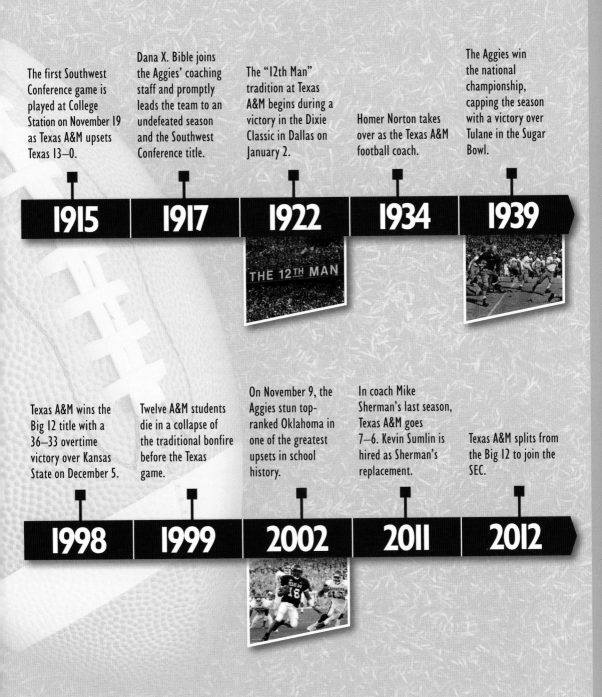

QUICK STATS

PROGRAM INFO
Agricultural and Mechanical College of
Texas Aggies (1903–62)
Texas A&M Aggies (1963–)

NATIONAL CHAMPIONSHIP
1939

OTHER ACHIEVEMENTS
BCS bowl appearances (1999–): 1
Southwest Conference
championships (1915–95): 17
Big 12 championships (1996–2011): 1
Bowl record: 14–19

HEISMAN TROPHY WINNERS
John David Crow, 1957

KEY PLAYERS
(POSITION[S]; SEASONS WITH TEAM)
Joe Boyd (OT; 1937–39)
John David Crow (RB; 1955–57)
Curtis Dickey (RB; 1976–79)
Lester Hayes (FS; 1973–76)
John Kimbrough (FB; 1938–40)
Darren Lewis (RB; 1987–90)
Von Miller (OLB; 2007–10)

* All statistics through 2011 season

Terrence Murphy (WR; 2001–04)
Dat Nguyen (LB; 1995–98)
Jack Pardee (FB/LB; 1954–56)
Ryan Tannehill (QB; 2008–11)

KEY COACHES
Dana X. Bible (1917; 1919–28):
72–19–9; 1–0 (bowl games)
Homer Norton (1934–47):
82–53–9; 2–2 (bowl games)
R. C. Slocum (1989–2002):
123–47–2; 3–8 (bowl games)

HOME STADIUM
Kyle Field (1927–)

Aggie Muster is one of Texas A&M's most revered traditions. It is celebrated every April 21. On this day, former students gather to link the past with the future and remember their fallen comrades. "If there is an A&M man in 100 miles of you, you are expected to get together, eat a little, and live over the days you spent at the A&M College of Texas," said a former Aggie student in 1923.

It was hardly an impressive start. Texas A&M was facing Southern Methodist in 1955. Aggies sophomore running back John David Crow gathered in a punt at his own 40-yard line. He promptly lost 30 yards trying to run along the outside of the Mustangs' defense. A few plays later, he lost another five yards on a sweep. The embarrassed Crow returned to the sidelines. He was expecting to be yelled at by coach Paul "Bear" Bryant. Instead, Bryant merely informed him, "John, our goal is that-a-way."

Maroon and white are the official Aggies colors. Certain games are designated as "Maroon Outs." Fans wear maroon clothing to show their Aggies spirit.

The military life at Texas A&M turns out commissioned officers for all of the military services. In fact, it extends to both the students and the animals. Reveille, the collie mascot for the Texas A&M football team, is commissioned as a five-star general and is the highest-ranking member of the Corps of Cadets.

GLOSSARY

athletic director

An administrator who oversees the coaches, players, and teams of an institution.

bowl game

A game after the season that teams earn the right to play in by having a good record.

conference

In sports, a group of teams that play each other each season.

deficit

The amount by which a team trails another team.

legend

An extremely famous person, especially in a particular field.

ranking

A national position as determined by voters.

recruited

To have enticed a player to come to a certain school to play on its football team. A player being sought after is known as a recruit.

retired

Officially ended one's career.

rivalry

When opposing teams bring out great emotion in each team, its fans, and its players.

scandal

A disgraceful incident.

upset

A game in which the team expected to lose emerges victorious.

varsity

The main team that represents a school.

FOR MORE INFORMATION

FURTHER READING

Burson, Rusty. *What It Means to be an Aggie: John David Crow and Texas A&M's Greatest Players.* Chicago: Triumph Books, 2010.

Herskowitz, Mickey. *The 1939 Texas Aggies: The Greatest Generation's Greatest Team.* Houston, TX: Halcyon Press, 2006.

Jacobs, Homer, and Rusty Burson. *Standing Together: The Spirit of Kyle Field.* Nashville, TN: Booksmith Group, 2008.

WEB LINKS

To learn more about the Texas A&M Aggies, visit ABDO Publishing Company online at **www.abdopublishing.com**. Web sites about the Aggies are featured on our Book Links page. These links are routinely monitored and updated to provide the most current information available.

PLACES TO VISIT

College Football Hall of Fame
111 South St. Joseph St.
South Bend, IN 46601
1-800-440-FAME (3263)
www.collegefootball.org

This Hall of Fame and Museum highlights the greatest players, coaches, and moments in the history of college football. Among the former Aggies enshrined are John David Crow and coach Dana X. Bible.

Kyle Field
198 Joe Routt Boulevard
College Station, TX 77840
979-845-5129
www.aggieathletics.com/ ViewArticle.dbml?DB_OEM_ ID=27300&ATCLID=205237869

As a complete stadium since 1927, Kyle Field is known as the Home of the "12th Man" and the Texas A&M Aggies.

INDEX

ABOUT THE AUTHOR

Ken Rappoport is a professional sportswriter with more than 50 books to his credit in both the adult and young readers' fields. Working for the Associated Press in New York for 30 years, he wrote about every major sport and was the AP's national hockey writer for 14 seasons. Along with the Stanley Cup playoffs and NHL All-Star Games, he covered the World Series, the Olympic Games, the Final Four, and the NBA Finals, among other assignments. Rappoport has been cited for his work in the young adult field and has written extensively for magazines.